Quiet Treasures

ECONOMY READING SERIES

Louise Matteoni
Floyd Sucher
Marvin Klein
Karen Welch

THE ECONOMY COMPANY

Oklahoma City
Indianapolis
Los Angeles

Cover Illustration: Linda Edwards

This text was developed with the assistance of Kraft & Kraft.

Permission to use or adapt copyrighted materials appearing in
this book is gratefully acknowledged on page 207, which
is hereby made a part of this copyright page.

ISBN 0-8332-2542-1

THE ECONOMY COMPANY, Educational Publishers
1200 Northwest 63rd Street
Oklahoma City, Oklahoma 73116-5712

    4 5 6 7 8 9 10 — 90 89 88 87 86

Contents

Animals

Daydreams

Nearby

Questions

Puzzles

Tick Tock Clock

When Will the Show Be On?

ANIMALS

A Lion Is a Big Cat

New Words

1. The birds have a nest on a branch of this tree.
2. Soon we will eat.
3. The paper has spots of red paint on it.
4. Where is the cat?

A Lion Is a Big Cat

Benjamin Khan

This is a nice little cat.
You can pat it.
A lion is a cat.
You see a lion in a zoo.
A lion is a big cat.

   Where can you go to see a big
cat?
Go to a zoo.
That is where you can see a lion.

   A lion is a big cat.
A little lion has spots.
A little lion will get big.
Then it will not have spots.

This big cat is not a lion.
It can make a noise like a lion.
The zoo has a pond for this big
cat.
Soon the cat will swim in the
pond.
Then it will get up on the shore.
That is where it will eat.

You can see the spots on this
big cat.
The spots are black.

The cat with spots will soon
sleep in a tree.
Soon this cat will get up in the
tree.
That is where it will sleep.
It will sleep on a branch.
It will stay on the branch and not
fall.

Can you see the cat with spots
up on the branch?
This cat is quick.
It can jump on food that it sees.

Answer these questions.
1. Where can you go to see a
   big cat?
2. Where will the cat with spots
   sleep?

What Made That Noise?

New Words

1. It was <u>just</u> the tree that made that noise.
2. Did the <u>clock</u> stop?
3. Please put the quilt on the <u>bed</u>.
4. Can you see the <u>puppy</u>?
5. It is <u>under</u> the tree.

What Made That Noise?

Lewis L. Symonds

"I can't sleep," Ann said.
"What was that noise?
Kate, please help me find what
made that noise."

"It was just the clock," Kate
said.
"The clock made the noise."

"It was not the clock," Ann
said.
"What was that noise, Kate?"

"I can't sleep," Ann said.
"Please help me find what made
the noise."

"It was just that tree," Kate
said.
"Please get back into bed and go
to sleep, Ann."

"It was not the tree," Ann
said.

"Where is the puppy?
Maybe it was just the puppy,"
Kate said.

"Maybe the puppy did make
that noise," Ann said.
"It was like a puppy noise.
The puppy was on the bed.
Where did the puppy go?
Did it go under the bed?
Let's look under the bed."

"Here is what made the noise,
Kate!
Look under the bed!" Ann said.
"The puppy is here, and it has
the ball!"

"The noise will stop soon,"
Kate said.

"The puppy will not play with
the ball.

The puppy will go to sleep.

Please get back into bed, Ann.

You can go to sleep like the
puppy."

Answer these questions.

1. What made Ann not sleep?
2. What is a puppy noise like?

Look at the Animals

New Words

1. <u>Point</u> to the bike that you want.
2. I want the bike that is on this <u>page</u>.
3. <u>Some</u> eggs are in the nest.
4. A puppy and a frog are <u>animals</u>.
5. I see just <u>one</u> duck.

Look at the Animals

Daniel Lewis

Fish can swim.
Some animals that are not fish
can swim, too.
Each of the animals you see here
can swim.
Just one of them is a fish.
Point to the animals that are not
fish.

Animals can make noise.
Some animals can make a big
noise.
Some animals can make a little
noise.
Point to the animals that make a
big noise.
Find the animals that make a little
noise.

Some big animals can jump.
Some little animals can jump, too.
Look at the animals on this page.
One of the animals on this page
can't jump.
Point to the one that can't jump.

Some animals can be quick.
Look at the animals on this page.
One of them is not quick.
Point to the one that is not quick.

Animals can be big.

Animals can be little.

Animals can make a big noise.

Animals can make just a little noise.

Animals can be quick.
They can jump, too.
Fish can swim.
Animals that are not fish can
swim, too.

Answer these questions.
1. What animals can make a big
   noise?
2. What big animals can jump?

That Seal!

New Words

1. Let's <u>walk</u> to the park.
2. That man has just one <u>child</u>.
3. Big and little fish are in the <u>sea</u>.
4. The <u>seal</u> will eat fish.
5. I <u>saw</u> a blue boat.

That Seal!

Jeanette Cook

This is Kate.
Each day Kate will walk on
the shore.
It is fun to walk with Kate.
Some people go to Kate for help.
One day a child came to Kate.

"Please help me," said
the child.
"I can't find the red ball."

"Did the ball fall into the
sea?" said Kate.

"The ball did not fall into
the sea," said the child.
"It was on the shore."

"Let's go for a walk on
the shore," said Kate.

Kate and the child went
up on a hill.
Then Kate saw the red ball.

"Look," said Kate.
"That seal has the ball."

The child said, "Seal,
please bring me the ball."

The seal saw Kate and
the child.
It did not bring the ball to them.
It made a funny noise and stayed
in the sea.
Kate and the child went to a shop.
They came back with a fish.
The seal saw the fish.

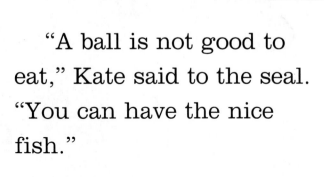

"A ball is not good to eat," Kate said to the seal. "You can have the nice fish."

The seal came to Kate to get the good fish.

"You may have the fish," Kate said to the seal. "And we will take the ball!"

Answer these questions.
1. What had the red ball?
2. What did Kate do to get the red ball?

The Furry Ones

I like
the furry ones—
the waggy ones
the purry ones
the hoppy ones
that hurry,

The glossy ones
the saucy ones
the sleepy ones
the leapy ones
the mousy ones
that scurry,

The snuggly ones
the hug-ly ones
the never, never
ugly ones . . .
all soft
and warm
and furry.

Aileen Fisher

35

DAYDREAMS

Two Angry Cats

New Words

1. Birds and <u>cats</u> are animals.
2. Please stop those <u>noises</u> so the child can sleep.
3. We <u>ate</u> fish and bread.
4. I saw <u>two</u> animals.
5. The cat was <u>angry</u>.

Two Angry Cats

Lewis L. Symonds

One day, two cats went for a
walk to find food.
One cat was black, and one cat
had spots.
"I see bread, and I will eat it!"
said the cat with spots.

"No," said the black cat.
"That bread is for me."
The cats made angry noises.
"I want it!" said the black cat.

"So do I!" said the cat with
spots.

The cats went to see the king.
"Maybe I can help," the king
said.
"Let's look at this bread.
It is too big for two cats, so I will
eat some of it."
He ate some of the bread.
"Here is some bread for you," he
said.

The cats made angry noises.
"I want it!" said the cat with
spots.

"No, I want it!" said the black
cat.
"I will take it!"

"I will help," said the king.
"The bread is too big for you."
He ate some of the bread.
"Here is some bread for you," he
said.

It was just a little bread, so
the cats made angry noises.
"I want it!" said the cat with
spots.
"I do!" said the black cat.

"You can't have it," the king
said to the two cats.
"I will eat it."
And the king ate the bread.
The two cats did not eat that day.
What did the king teach them?

Answer these questions.
1. What did the cats find?
2. What made the cats make
   angry noises?

The Gold Goose

1. <u>When</u> can we go to the zoo?
2. Please <u>let</u> me go with you.
3. I can't find <u>my</u> toy boat.
4. The duck and the <u>goose</u> are birds.
5. The funny puppy made me <u>smile</u>.
6. The man and his <u>wife</u> like animals.
7. Put the ball in his <u>hand</u>.
8. Do not <u>touch</u> the lion.

The Gold Goose

Susan DeStefano

A good child went to the park
to eat his bread.
A man said, "Please let me have
some of that bread."
So the good child did.
The man said, "You are so good
to me that I want you to have my
gold goose."

One day, the child said, "I want to see the princess with no smile.
Maybe my gold goose will make her smile."

On the way, the good child saw a tall man and his wife.
The tall man saw the gold goose.

"Let me have that goose," the
tall man said.

"Do not touch my goose," the
good child said.
The tall man did touch it.
When he did, his hand stayed on
the goose.

"Help!" the man said to his
wife.
"The goose won't let me go!"
When his wife went to help the
man, her hand stayed on his back.

So the man and his wife had to
go with the good child to make
the princess smile.
On the way, they saw Big Bill.

"Help!" the tall man said.
"The goose won't let me and my
wife go."
Then he said, "Do not touch my
wife."
Big Bill had just put his hand on
her hat.
His hand stayed on her hat.

47

The good child said, "We will go to see the princess just like this.
This will make her smile."
And when the princess saw them, just like that, she did smile.

Answer these questions.
1. What did the good child want to do for the princess?
2. What made the princess smile?

The Three Wishes

New Words

1. <u>Why</u> did you do that?
2. We saw <u>an</u> old lion when we went to the zoo.
3. The little <u>elf</u> had a green hat.
4. Ned <u>gave</u> a plant to Ann.
5. She had a plant for <u>him</u>, too.
6. The <u>woman</u> made a wish.
7. One and two are <u>three</u>.
8. I wish I had two <u>wishes</u>.

The Three Wishes

Elizabeth West

One day a woman went to a
shop to get some bread.
Then the woman saw an elf.
The elf said, "Please feed me.
I have no food."

The woman gave the bread to
him.
The elf ate it.
Then he said, "You gave me food,
so you may have three wishes."

The woman came back with no bread.

The man said, "Where is the bread?"

The woman said, "I gave the bread to an elf."

The man said, "Why did you let him have the bread?"

The woman said, "He had no food.
So I gave him the bread.
Then the elf gave me three wishes."

The man said, "I like gold.
Let's wish for a gold ring."

The woman said, "I wish that I
had a big fish to eat."

The woman had her wish.
A big fish came to her.

The man was angry.
He said, "Why did you wish for
that?
An elf gave you three wishes.
You can wish for gold!
You can wish for me to be a
king!
What do you wish for?
You wish for a fish!
I wish that you had the fish on
you!" he said.

The man had his wish.
The fish was on the woman, and
it stayed on her.

The woman said, "Why did you wish for that?
People will point at me and smile.
I wish that I did not have this fish on me."

The man and woman had made three wishes.
They had no fish and no wishes.

Answer these questions.
1. What did the woman wish for?
2. Why was the man angry with the woman?

Who Made the Lion Smile?

New Words

1. I like to play with my <u>toys</u>.
2. That big <u>pile</u> of paper may fall.
3. Rosa wants to go, <u>but</u> I do not.
4. Bill <u>got</u> some food for the duck.
5. <u>Someone</u> is in the van.
6. <u>There</u> are some animals.
7. Is he the man <u>who</u> has the toy shop?
8. The cat had <u>kittens</u>.

Who Made the Lion Smile?

Katherine Talmadge

There was a man who had a
toy shop.
Each day he went to his shop.
His cat went there, too.
The man made toys.
One day he made a toy lion.
It was a nice toy, but it had
an angry look.

"Who will want this toy?"
the man said to his cat.
"I wish that I had made a lion
with a smile, but I did not."

He put the lion in his shop.
When people came to the shop,
they got toys.
Someone got a red truck.
Someone got a big green frog.
But the lion stayed in the shop.
No one came for a lion with an
angry look.
So the man put it in a pile of toys
in back of the shop.

One day the cat had kittens.
The man made a little nest for the
cat and her kittens.
He put an old quilt in back of the
shop for them.
The pile of toys was there, too.
The lion was in the pile of toys.

Two of the kittens did not want
to stay in the nest.
So they went to play in the pile of
toys.
The man went to find the kittens.
"Here they are," the man said.
"They are with the angry lion.
Maybe they want to be with this
toy that no one wants."

When the man saw the lion, it made him jump back.

The lion did not have an angry look.

The lion had a big smile!

Who made the lion smile?

It was the two little kittens.

The lion had to have someone to want him.

And the little kittens did want him!

Answer these questions.

1. Why did the man make a nest for the kittens?

2. Where did the little kittens go?

The Big Black Bear

New Words

1. An old tree is <u>by</u> the pond.
2. Pete has a black cat and a <u>white</u> cat.
3. I am <u>glad</u> to do that for you.
4. The child gave me a <u>kiss</u>.
5. "May I play with you?" said <u>Ed</u>.
6. We saw <u>Kim</u> when we went to the park.
7. <u>Grandmother</u> gave me a dog.
8. When did Kate get back <u>from</u> the shop?
9. I saw a <u>bear</u> and a lion at the zoo.

The Big Black Bear

Emilie Ferry

I went to stay with
Grandmother.
She was glad to see me.
She gave me a kiss.

Grandmother said, "We
will have fun, Ed.
There is a big park here."

"People play in the park.
Someone is there to help the
people.
You will like to play there,
too."

Grandmother said, "I will
stay here and paint.
I will see where you go.
Soon I will be there, too."

So I went to the park.
But I did not want to stay.

I went back to Grandmother.

She said, "Why are you
back from the park?"

"It is too big," I said.
"And a wild bear is there!"

"A bear?" said Grandmother.
"Where is the bear?"

"It is by a tree," I said.
"It is big and black. 'Go get
the bear,' someone said."

"I want to see that bear,"
said Grandmother.
"Let's go look for it."

Grandmother and I went
to the park.

"See?" I said.
"It is by the tree.
It is big and black."

Grandmother said, "I see
it, too.
But it is not a bear.
It is a big, black dog.
And it has a little, white,
toy bear."

Someone said, "I am Kim.
Big Black is my dog."

Grandmother said, "This
is Ed.
We are glad to see you."

I said, "Where did the
dog get the white bear?"

"It came from a toy
shop," said Kim.
"It is a toy for Big Black."

Big Black put his white
bear by me.

"He wants you to take
the white bear from him.
He wants you to play with
him," said Kim.

"He gave you a kiss, Ed.
Do you like to get a kiss
from Big Black?
Do you want to play with
Big Black and me?"

"I do want to play.
I do want to play with you,"
I said.
"I like the park.
I am glad to be here."

Answer these questions.
1. Who said, "Go get
   the bear"?
2. What did Grandmother
   want to see?
3. Why did the dog kiss Ed?

Mr. Pyme

Once upon a time
Old Mr. Pyme
Lived all alone
Under a stone.

When the rain fell
He rang a bell,
When the sun shined
He laughed and dined

And floated to town
On thistledown,
And what a nice time
Had Mr. Pyme!

Harry Behn

Stop and Go

Look this way and that way.
Do you see a truck?
Do not walk.
Stay where you are.
The truck will stop.
Then you can walk.

NEARBY

Travel in the City

New Words

1. It is fun to <u>travel</u> in a van.
2. That <u>bus</u> will take them to the fish shop.
3. The <u>road</u> went up a hill.
4. Some people are in the <u>city</u>.
5. Please <u>come</u> with me.
6. We will ride in the <u>car</u>.

Travel in the City

Daniel Lewis

People travel to the city each day.
They come by car, by bus, by train.
Some people come to the city in a van that is made just for them.

When people travel to the city
by car, they drive on a road.
When they travel by bus, they
ride on a road, too.
When they come by train, they do
not go on the road where the car
and bus go.
They ride under the road.

People like to walk in the city,
too.
They like to walk to the park.

There is a zoo in the city, but
some people can't find the way.
There are people in the city who
can help them.

That woman will help the
people find the zoo.
She will point the way for them.
The people can travel by bus to
get to the zoo.
They can travel by train, too.

Those people came to the city
in a car.
They want to shop.
They can go to a toy shop.
They will not have to drive the car
to get there.
They can walk to the shop.

This man came to the city in a
big truck.
The truck has food in it.
The man will drive the truck to a
food shop.

The city is so big that people can do what they like to do.
They can drive a truck.
They can shop.
They can go to the zoo.
They can walk in the park.
They can sit under a tree and see the people who come to the city each day.

Answer this question.
In what do people come to the city?

What Will We Do Today?

New Words

1. I put the puppy in the box, but it got <u>out</u>.
2. I have paper and <u>glue</u> to make a paper hat.
3. The paint is not <u>dry</u>.
4. <u>Today</u> they will be here.
5. There is just one <u>leaf</u> on that tree.
6. That is a <u>pretty</u> blue bird.
7. <u>Mr.</u> Green said, "Look at what I do."

What Will We Do Today?

Benjamin Khan

"What is in that big box?" said
Pat.
"I see white paper and glue.
I see some dry grass, too.
What can we do with dry grass?
White paper is not too pretty.
Do you have pretty paper?
I like red paper."

"You can make this white
paper pretty," Mr. Green said.
"Today I will teach you what to
do.
Will you please take the glue out
of the box?" said Mr. Green.
"This is white glue.
Please take the grass and the
paper out of the box, too."

"Put a little glue on the grass.
Then put the grass on the paper.
Maybe I will put some tall grass
here," Mr. Green said.
"That looks nice.
Let the glue dry.
The grass will stay on the paper
and make it look pretty."

"Look at that red leaf.
It is so pretty!" Pat said.
"May I take this leaf out of the
box?
Maybe I can put this leaf on my
paper with the grass.
The leaf is dry, so I can glue it.
Then the paper will have a little
red on it, too."

Pat said, "Look at what I made today!
Do we have glue and white paper?
I can teach you to make paper like this today!"

Answer this question.

What can you do to make paper pretty?

Are Pets That Nice?

New Words

1. I have to <u>wash</u> the quilt that has paint on it.
2. Do not be <u>afraid</u> of animals.
3. Rosa has to find a good <u>home</u> for the kittens.
4. My red dress is <u>clean</u>, but my green dress has paint on it.
5. A cat is a nice <u>pet</u>.
6. A dog and a fish are nice <u>pets</u>, too.
7. Is this <u>your</u> cat?
8. We have a <u>new</u> car.

Are Pets That Nice?

Benjamin Khan

"I like your new home.
It is so pretty," Bill said.
"You have a tree in your home!
I wish we had one.
Is that your cat?
It is so big.
Do not let it jump on me.
I am clean, and I want to stay clean.
I do not like pets."

"My cat won't jump on you.
Cats are clean animals.
They wash and wash.
A cat is a good pet," said Rosa.
"My cat is nice, and she is pretty,
too.
She has three new kittens.
Do you want to see them?
They are so little.
When they get big, I have to find
a new home for them.
Do you want one for a pet?"

"I do not want one!
I do not like pets!
I am afraid of them when they get
big," said Bill.
"I do not want a pet.
It will get big.
I am afraid of your big cat, but I
am not afraid of little kittens.
I want to see them."

Bill said, "Look at those pretty little kittens!

One is white, one is black, and one is gold.

Let's not make noise, so they can sleep.

Kittens are nice, but big cats are not.

Maybe I will touch one of the kittens.

I am not afraid of them."

"Do not be afraid of big cats.
This big cat is nice.
Just look at her wash her new
kittens," Rosa said.
"She will wash each one.
She will feed them and clean
them.
She will play with them when they
get big.
They will jump on her and take
her food, but she will be nice to
them."

"Are cats that nice?" said Bill.
"Maybe your big cat is nice.
Maybe she is not angry.
She may just look that way.
She is nice to the kittens.
May I touch one?
Will it be afraid of me?
Will the big cat be angry?
She is not angry, is she?
She let me touch her kittens.
Maybe I am not so afraid of big
cats."

"I am not afraid of your big cat!" Bill said.

"I do want one of the kittens for a pet.

Pets are nice!"

Answer this question.

Why is Bill afraid that the big cat will be angry?

Pete, the Wet Pet

New Words

1. Please come to my <u>house</u>.
2. The dog has paint on his <u>feet</u>.
3. He has some on his <u>tail</u>, too.
4. When paint <u>gets</u> on the quilt, we have to wash it.
5. The road is <u>wet</u>.
6. That woman <u>comes</u> to this park each day.
7. The dog will <u>shake</u> to get dry.
8. Van <u>shakes</u> the tree to make the old nest fall.
9. This train <u>goes</u> to the city.
10. Please wash the <u>floor</u>.

Pete, the Wet Pet

Catherine Chase

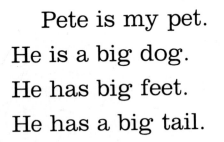

Pete is my pet.
He is a big dog.
He has big feet.
He has a big tail.

He goes out and gets wet.
Then he comes home to get dry.
When Pete comes home wet, he
shakes and gets the house wet.

96

When he comes into the
house, he goes shake, shake,
shake.
He gets the floor wet.

He goes shake, shake, shake
there.
He gets that floor wet.

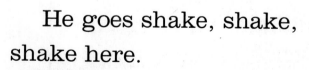

He goes shake, shake,
shake here.
He gets this floor wet, too.

My mom comes into the
house.
Pete is glad to see my mom, so
he shakes his big tail.
His big tail is wet.
It gets my mom wet.

"Pete, you are a good dog.
But you are a big dog with big
feet.
You have a big tail, and you are
wet.
You are a wet pet!
Please make Pete dry."

I dry his big feet.
I dry his big tail.
I dry his big back.

"Pete, you are not a wet pet.
You are a dry pet."

Pete shakes his big dry
tail.

Answer these questions.
1. What gets Pete wet?
2. What gets the house wet?

Go Away, Dog

New Words

1. Did the man drive the truck <u>away</u> from here?
2. Bill has two cats and two <u>dogs</u>.
3. Will the puppy bring the <u>stick</u> to me?
4. <u>If</u> you go to the city, I will go with you.
5. Pat wants to <u>run</u> in the race.
6. Please do not drive the car too <u>fast</u>.
7. I <u>don't</u> see you.
8. Can you <u>throw</u> a ball?

Go Away, Dog

Joan L. Nodset

Go away, you old dog.
Go away from me.
I don't like you, dog.
I don't like dogs.
I don't like big dogs, little
dogs, black dogs, white
dogs.

I don't want that stick.
Do you want me to throw the
stick?
If I throw the stick, will you
go away?

There, go away with your
stick.

Why did you come back?
What do you want?
If I throw the stick, will you go away?

Don't jump on me, dog.
I don't like that.
Go away, you old dog.
Go on home.

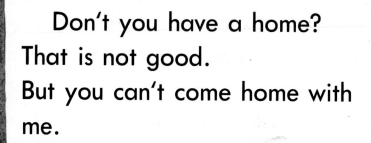

Don't you have a home?
That is not good.
But you can't come home with me.

Don't shake your tail at me.
I don't like dogs.
You are nice for a dog.
But I don't like dogs.

Can you shake my hand?
This is the way to shake.

Stop that, you old dog.
If I play with you, will you go
away?

Let's run, dog.
Can you run fast?
You can run fast!
You are a fast dog.

That was good, dog.
Maybe we can play on a new
day.
But I have to go home.

108

No, you can't come.
Go away, dog.

Don't look like that, dog.
Don't look that way at me.
Can I help it if you don't have
a home?
Why don't you go away?

You like me, don't you,
you old dog?
I like you, too.
You win, dog.
Come on home, dog.
Come on, let's run.

Answer these questions.
1. What did the dog bring to the child?
2. Did the child like the dog?
3. Why did the child take the dog home?

113

You

I like shadows
I like sun
I like you
more than anyone.

I like summer
I like the cold
I'll even like you
when you're old.

I like work
I like play
I like you
every which way.

Charlotte Zolotow

Do Not Touch

You may see this on a can in your house.

You may see this on a can in your house.

What do you do if you see those?
Stay away!
Don't touch!
What is in the can is not good for you.
Stay away!
Don't touch!

QUESTIONS

Water Birds and Black Oil

New Words

1. <u>How</u> did the bird get out of the cage?
2. The kittens eat, and then the cat <u>washes</u> them.
3. The bird will teach the little birds to <u>fly</u>.
4. The boat <u>sank</u>.
5. May I help you put the <u>oil</u> in your car?
6. Can you clean the floor with this <u>soap</u>?
7. <u>Water</u> birds like to eat fish.
8. Let's go to the park <u>again</u>.

Water Birds and Black Oil

Susan DeStefano

Water birds like the sea.
They like to eat the fish that are
in the water.
They like to fly in and out of the
water.

One day, a big boat sank into
the sea.
When the boat sank, black oil
came out of the boat.
The oil stayed on the water.

When the boat sank, the ugly
black oil went onto the water.
The oil got on the birds.
That was not good for the water
birds.

Birds can't fly in and out of
the water if they have black oil
on them.
The oil got on the fish, too.
So the birds had no fish to eat.

People came to see the black
oil on the water.
They saw that the oil was on
the birds, too.

The people saw that the birds
did not fly.
They saw that the birds had no
fish to eat.
The people had to help the birds.

How did the people help?
They had to take the birds out of
the water.
Then they gave the birds clean
water.

The people had to wash the
birds.
How did they wash them?
They put them into soap and
water.
They had to wash the birds again
and again to get them clean.

This is how she washes the
duck.
She washes the duck in soap and
water.
She washes the duck again and
again to get it clean.

The black oil that is on the
duck will go into the soap and
water.

When the duck is clean, she
can dry it.
The duck is clean and dry.

Water birds have to have some oil on them.

This is a clean oil that the birds make.

The soap had made the birds too clean.

There was no black oil on them, and there was no clean oil on them.

The birds had to make new oil.
The birds had to have some food
and some sleep, too.
The people gave the birds food.
They let them sleep.
They let the birds make the oil
that they had to have.
Then the people let the birds
fly back to the sea.

Answer these questions.

1. What do water birds like to eat?
2. How did black oil get on the birds?
3. How did people clean the birds?

Sea Frog, City Frog

New Words

1. The frog <u>hopped</u> up the hill.
2. Fish and <u>frogs</u> are in this pond.
3. My dog can walk on her back <u>legs</u>.
4. Tom <u>wanted</u> to shop, but Rosa did not.
5. The puppy has a wet <u>nose</u>.
6. What <u>would</u> you like to do?
7. They <u>were</u> at the zoo.
8. A lion has a <u>long</u> tail.

Sea Frog, City Frog

Dorothy O. Van Woerkom

Sea Frog had his home by the sea.

City Frog had his home in a pond in the city.

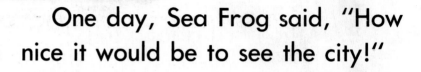

One day, Sea Frog said, "How nice it would be to see the city!"

And City Frog said, "I would like to see the sea!"

So City Frog hopped out of his
pond.
He hopped on the way to the sea.

And Sea Frog hopped out of
his home.
He hopped on the way to the city.

The two frogs hopped for a
day.
Then they came to a hill.
Up the hill hopped City Frog.
Up the hill hopped Sea Frog.

Sea Frog saw City Frog.
City Frog saw Sea Frog.

"I am from the city," said City
Frog.
"I am on my way to the sea.
Where are you from?
Where do you want to go?"

Sea Frog said, "I am from the
sea.
I am on my way to the city."

"How nice to see you,"
said City Frog.
"Let's sit."
So they did.

Then City Frog said, "I wish that we were tall."

Sea Frog said, "What good would it do if we were tall? Would it get you to the sea and me to the city?"

"No," said City Frog. "But here we are on this hill. If we were tall, we would see a long way."

"We can do it!" Sea Frog said. "We can be tall."

"How can we do that?" said
City Frog.

"Like this," said Sea Frog.
Sea Frog got up on his long back
legs.
"We have long back legs.
We can be tall if we do this!"

So each frog got up on his
long back legs.

"I can see a long way!" said
City Frog.

"So can I," Sea Frog said.

City Frog wanted to see the sea.
So his nose was to the sea.
And Sea Frog wanted to see the city.
So his nose was to the city.

Each frog put his nose to where he wanted to go.
But the frogs just saw where they had come from!

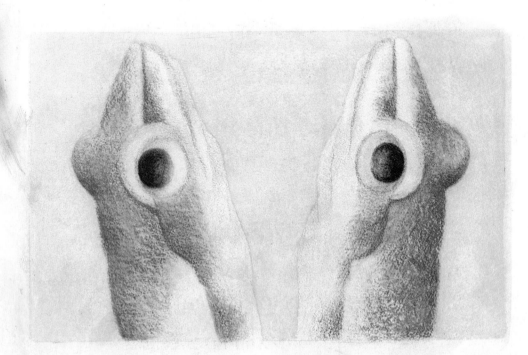

"The city is just like the sea!" said Sea Frog.

"The sea is just like the city!" said City Frog.

So the frogs went home again. And they did not find out that the sea is not like the city and the city is not like the sea.

Answer these questions.

1. What did Sea Frog want to see?
2. What did City Frog want to see?
3. Did the frogs get what they wanted?

Chicken Forgets

New Words

1. If you go to a <u>farm</u>, you may see a duck, a hen, and a goose.
2. A <u>weed</u> is a plant.
3. "<u>Chicken</u>, I want your help," said the hen.
4. <u>All</u> the toys are new.
5. What did you <u>say</u> to me?
6. She is my <u>mother</u>.
7. Do you like to eat <u>berries</u>?
8. Put the food in the <u>basket</u>.
9. I won't <u>forget</u> you.
10. We went <u>across</u> the road.

Chicken Forgets

Miska Miles

"Chicken," the mother hen
said, "I want your help.
I want you to get berries.
I want a basket of wild berries."

"I would like to get berries,"
the little chicken said.

"Take this basket for the
berries," the mother hen said.
"Please, please, don't forget the
berries."

"I won't forget," the little
chicken said.
"I will look for wild berries."

He went across the grass.
He did not want to forget.
So he said again and again, "Get
wild berries.
Get wild berries."

All the way to the pond, he
said, "Get wild berries."

Then the chicken saw an old frog.

"What did you say?" the frog said.

"Get wild berries," the chicken said.

"Don't say that to me," the frog said.

"What do you want me to say?" said the chicken.

"Get a big green fly," the frog said.

The chicken went on his way
across the grass.
He did not want to forget.
So he said, "Get a big green fly.
Get a big green fly."

All the way to the farm, he
said, "Get a big green fly."

At the farm, he saw a sheep.
"Don't say that to ME," the sheep
said.

"What do you want me to
say?" said the chicken.

"Get a green weed,"
said the sheep.

On the chicken went, by the
farm.
He said again and again, "Get a
green weed.
Get a green weed."

"No, no," said a bird.
"Berries are what you want.
Come with me."

So the little chicken went with
the bird.
Soon he saw wild berries.

The bird came and ate
and ate.
And the little chicken put
wild berries in his basket.

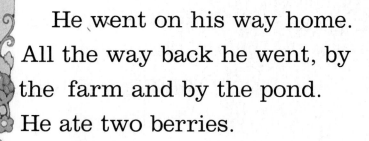

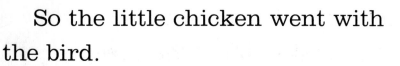

He went on his way home.
All the way back he went, by
the farm and by the pond.
He ate two berries.

Across the grass he went.
And he ate three berries.

At home, the mother hen
saw the berries.
"You did not forget," she said.
"You did bring home berries.
I am so glad!
You are a good little chicken."

And the little chicken was
glad, too.

Answer these questions.
1. Why did the chicken go to the
   pond and the farm?
2. What did the frog want the
   chicken to say?
3. What did the sheep want the
   chicken to say?

Where Is Baby Cow?

New Words

1. Ned <u>didn't</u> want to go, but he had to.
2. We <u>waited</u> for them, but they did not come.
3. Kate <u>looked</u> for the ball, but she did not find it.
4. The bus went up and <u>down</u> the hill each day.
5. Mother <u>Cow</u> had to help clean the farm.
6. They had to clean <u>their</u> house.
7. "Please feed me," said Baby <u>Bird</u>.
8. I <u>could</u> not see the play.
9. I <u>know</u> who you are.

Where Is Baby Cow?

Daniel Lewis

It was the day to clean the farm.
All the animals stayed home to wash and clean.
The goose had to wash out his big black pot.
The chicken had to get some clean, dry grass for her floor.
The birds had to take down their nest to shake it out.

Each house on the farm would
soon be clean.
That is, all but one house would
soon be clean.

Mother Cow had a big house.
It was too big for just her to
clean.
"Baby Cow will have to help me,"
she said.
"Baby Cow, come and help."
But Baby Cow didn't come.

141

Mother Cow waited and waited
and waited.
"I will look for Baby Cow," she
said.
She looked under the old farm
truck.
She didn't find him there.
She looked down at the pond.
But she didn't find him there.

On the road, Mother Cow saw the farm kittens.
They had a big pile of wash to do.
"Did you see Baby Cow?" Mother Cow said to them.

"No, we didn't," they said.
"Maybe Baby Cow didn't want to clean your big house."

Mother Cow sank to the grass under a tree.
Her house was not clean.
She could not find Baby Cow.
"What *will* I do?" she said.

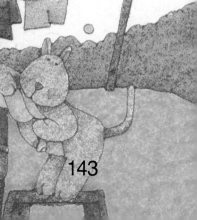

Just then, Big Red came by.
"Can I help?" she said.

"Do you know where Baby
Cow is?" Mother Cow said.

"Have you looked way down
the hill where the grass is tall?"
Big Red said.

"I know that Baby Cow would
not go there.
He would be afraid to travel
all that way," Mother Cow said.

"Let's just walk down there
and see," Big Red said.

It was a long walk.
When Mother Cow and Big
Red got to the tall grass, there
was Baby Cow.
He was glad to see them.

Mother Cow was a little angry,
but she was glad to see him, too.
"Why did you run away?" she
said to him.

"I didn't want to clean, so I came here.
Then I could not find my way back home.
I don't like it here.
Ugly noises made me afraid.
Please take me home.
I will be glad to help you clean," Baby Cow said.

So Baby Cow and Mother Cow
went home to clean their house.
Soon their big house was clean.
It was so clean that all of the
animals from the farm came to
see it.

"I know we won't soon forget this day, will we?" Mother Cow said to Baby Cow.
But Baby Cow could not say.

Answer these questions.
1. Where did Mother Cow look for Baby Cow?
2. Where was Baby Cow?
3. Why was the day a long day?

King and Princess

New Words

1. How <u>far</u> did the people travel by car?
2. Will the puppy sit on my <u>lap</u>?
3. <u>King's</u> house is clean.
4. We <u>climbed</u> up the hill.
5. We got <u>off</u> the bus.
6. The bird <u>flew</u> away.
7. What is on your <u>head</u>?

King and Princess

Gari Fairweather

Rosa has two pets, King and
Princess.

King is a dog.
He is all black from his head to
his tail.

Princess is a bird.
She is all green from her head to
her tail.

One day Rosa got some paper
and paint.

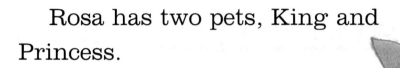

King wanted to be with Rosa.
He wanted to see Rosa paint.
He climbed up onto her lap.

"Stay away, King," Rosa said
to him.
"Stay far away so I can paint."

King climbed off her lap.
King's head went down.
King's tail went down.

Off King went.
He didn't look happy at all.

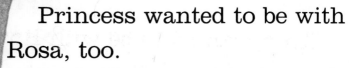

Princess wanted to be with
Rosa, too.
She wanted to see Rosa paint.
So Princess flew onto her lap.

"Stay away, Princess," Rosa
said to her.
"Stay far away so I can paint."

Princess flew off to King.
She didn't look happy at all.

King and Princess did not
want to stay away.
They wanted to see Rosa paint.

King came from the tree.
Princess flew off King's head.
They waited to see what Rosa
would say.

But Rosa did not see them.
She put some blue paint onto the
paper.

King came up to Rosa.
Princess hopped up to Rosa.
They waited to see what Rosa
would say.

But Rosa did not see them.
She put some white paint onto
the paper.

Just then King climbed
onto her lap.
Princess flew onto her head.

Up hopped Rosa!
Down went King and Princess.
Down went the white paint.

"Look at you!" said Rosa.

King looked at Princess.
She was green with white spots.

Princess looked at King.
He was black with white spots.

"You won't like this," Rosa
said to her pets.
"But I have to wash you off."

Princess wanted to fly away.
She did not like water at all.

King's head went down.
King's tail went down.
He did not like soap at all.

Rosa had to wash her pets
again and again.
And King and Princess did not
like that at all.

Rosa has two pets, King and Princess.

King is a dog.
He is all black again from his head to his tail.

Princess is a bird.
She is all green again from her head to her tail.

King and Princess like to be with Rosa.
But if Rosa wants to paint, they stay away.
They stay far, far away.

Answer these questions.

1. What do King and Princess like to do?

2. Why do King and Princess stay far away when Rosa wants to paint?

Is There a Place?

Is there a place where
shadows go
when it is
dark?

Do they play
in the
park?
Slip down slides?

Stride down streets?
Stretch high?
Shrink thin?

Do they spin
in the wind and
fly
with leaves?

Splash in the
rain?
Hang up to
dry?

Lilian Moore

What Do They Say?

What do they say?
Some say what you may do.
Some say what you may not do.
Some say where you may go.

PUZZLES

The Clue behind the Old Clock

New Words

1. Do you want fish <u>or</u> chicken?
2. Sam was <u>sad</u>, but today he is happy.
3. "<u>Hello</u>," Pete said.
4. Bill <u>hid</u> under the bed, and we could not find him.
5. This <u>clue</u> will help you find out where the gold is.
6. The baby <u>touches</u> the puppy with her hand.
7. I like <u>Grandma</u>.
8. My cat <u>does</u> not like water.
9. Look <u>behind</u> the tree.

The Clue
behind the Old Clock

Katherine Talmadge

Pat: Van, I see Grandma at her
food shop.
She looks sad.

Van: She does look sad.
Hello, Grandma!

Grandma: Hello, Pat and Van.

Man: Hello.

Grandma: Hello.
Do you want to sit out here or
in the shop?

Man: I will sit out here.
This shop was here when I was
a little child.
That old clock was here, too.

Grandma: I like my shop and the
old clock, but I have to go
back to the city.

Van: Why, Grandma?

Grandma: The shop is old.
I have to paint it, but I can't
pay for paint.

Man: That is sad.
When I was little, an old man
said that he hid gold here.

Pat: Where?

Man: No one can find the gold.

Van: Can we find it, Grandma?
Then you can pay for paint.

Grandma: What a nice wish!

Man: Maybe you can find where
the old man hid the gold.

Pat: Can we help you, Grandma?

Grandma: You can help me clean
the old clock.

Man: That clock was here when
the old man hid the gold.
Good day!

Grandma: Come back soon!
Van or Pat, please take the
old clock down.

Van: I will, Grandma.

Pat: Van, look!
    A paper was behind the clock!

Grandma: What is it?

Pat: It looks like a clue!
    Here is what is on the paper:
    "When my hand touches
    three, it will point to gold!"

Van: Gold!
    Does the clock point to gold?

Grandma: It IS a clue!
"When my hand touches
three, it will point to gold!"

Van: How can it point to gold?

Grandma: Let's make the big
hand point to three.
Then maybe we will see.

Pat: Where does the hand point?

Van: When the hand touches
three, it can point to that old
tree.

Grandma: Van or Pat, you look
in the tree.
I will look in the grass.

Van: I can't see gold here.

Grandma: It is not under or
behind the tree.

Pat: Look at this old box!
It was in the tree!

Van: What is in the box?

Pat: There is gold in the box!

Van: Grandma, you can pay for
paint with this gold!

Pat: We can help you paint!

Grandma: That would help me!

Van: We had a good clue.
The clue was behind the old
clock!

Answer this question.
How did the man in the shop
help Grandma?

What Will the Weather Be?

New Words

1. Please <u>turn</u> the clock so that I can see it.
2. We have to feed the birds that stay here each <u>winter</u>.
3. The <u>rain</u> will get you wet.
4. The <u>wind</u> will make the boat go.
5. Please <u>show</u> me how to do that.
6. Put a quilt on your bed so you won't be <u>cold</u>.
7. The <u>weather</u> is nice today.
8. The birds flew to a <u>high</u> branch.
9. You are <u>different</u> from me.

What Will the Weather Be?

Stanley Elvin

Can you say what the
weather will be?
Some people say they can
find out.

Some people look at birds.
They may see a bird fly
high out to sea.
Then they say it will be a
nice day.

Birds do not like to fly
out to sea when it could rain.
When the weather will be
bad, sea birds turn back
and stay on shore.

A big wind can come
with a rain.
Birds do not like to fly in a
big wind.
They may sit in a tree when
rain is on the way.

Some people look at
different animals on a farm.
A chicken may make a big
noise when rain is on the
way.
It may run here and there.
Sheep can show when it
will be cold.
They will stay this way
when it is cold.

A frog can show the
weather, too.
A tree frog will make a big
noise when rain is on the
way.
It will stay in the water.
On a nice day, it will not
make a big noise.
It will come up high out of
the water.

Some people say that different animals can show when the winter will be cold.
If wild animals make a good nest in the fall, a cold winter may come soon.
Some wild animals have a home on a high hill.
They come down when bad winter weather is on the way.

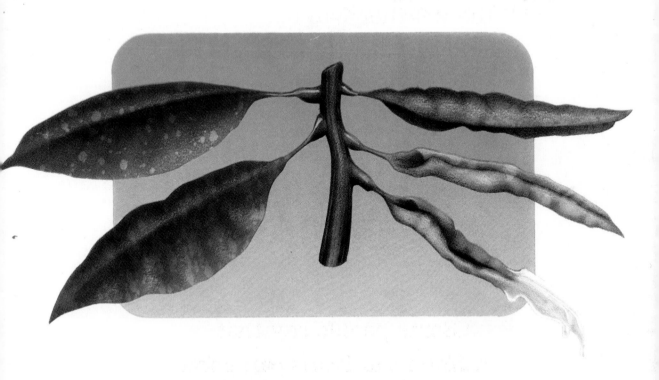

A big wind may come.
A big wind can make the
weather turn cold.
Wind can make people and
animals cold.
A plant can get cold, too.
Each leaf of this plant will
turn in when it is cold.

People like to know what the weather will be.

Some people find out when they see different birds or animals.

Some find out when they look at a plant.

Can you find out, too?

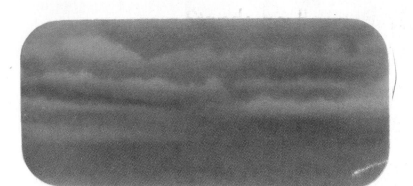

Answer these questions.

1. How do birds and animals show what the weather will be?

2. How does a leaf show how cold the weather is?

The Big Jump

New Words

1. Tom will bring one box and I will bring two <u>boxes</u>.
2. Is Pat tall or <u>short</u>?
3. Mr. Hill has one child and Mr. King has three <u>children</u>.
4. <u>Ben</u> wants me to go to his house to play.
5. Some birds made a nest on <u>top</u> of the old van.
6. The baby has little legs and feet, and she can take just a little <u>step</u>.
7. A <u>palace</u> is the home of a king.

The Big Jump

Benjamin Elkin

There was a day when no one
but a king could have a dog.
So the king had all the dogs.
He had big dogs and little dogs,
tall dogs and short dogs.

The king and his dogs would go
out to play.
Then the children would all come
to look at the king and his dogs.

182

One day, a dog went away
from the king.
It went to Ben.
Ben gave the dog a pat.

"Go back!" he said.
"I am not a king!
Go back to the king!"

But the dog would not go back
to the king.

"Look at that!" said the king.
"My dog does like you.
But you are not a king.
If you were a king, you could
have this dog."

"How I wish I could have it!"
said Ben.
"Could *I* be a king?
What do I have to do to be one?"

"A king has to know how to do
the Big Jump."

"The Big Jump?" said Ben.

But the king was not there!

Then Ben saw him way up high
on top of his palace!

"How did you get up there?"
said Ben.

"I did the Big Jump," said the
king.
"If *you* could jump up here, you
could have the dog!"

Then the king came back.
He looked down at Ben.

"Would you like to have that
dog?" he said.

"I would," said Ben.

"You may take him home with
you for one day," said the king.
"See how high you can jump.
Then come back.
If you can jump to the top of my
palace, you may have him."

186

"I will do what I can," said
Ben.
"I will go home and see how high
I can jump."

Ben could make a short jump.

He could jump to the top of
one box.

He could jump to the top of
two boxes.

But he could not jump to the
top of three boxes.

Then Ben got a big stick to
help him jump.
He could jump high.
He could jump to the top of three
boxes.

But that was all.

And then the dog made a short
jump.

The dog hopped up on one box.
From that box, he hopped to a new box.
When he got to the top box, he looked back at Ben.

"Good, good dog!" Ben said.
"I know how to do it!
The king will see that I can jump to the top of his palace."

Then Ben went back to see the
king.
The king was on top of his palace.

"I can do it!" said Ben to the
king.
"Like this!"

Ben went up one short step.
Then he went up a new short
step.
Jump, jump, jump.
Step by step to the top of the
palace.

The children looked at
Ben.
"We can *all* do it *that* way!"
the children said.

"You can all do it," said the
king.
"You know how, for you saw
Ben do it.
Ben did not have to do it in *one*
jump—and he did not.
But he did jump to the top.
So the dog is his."

Ben was so glad.

"You did it for me," Ben said
to the dog.
"I saw how you did it.
Then I did it.
You are JUMP.
And you will be my pet
from this day on!"

And that is how Ben came
to have a dog.

Answer these questions.
1. What people could have
   dogs?
2. What did Ben have to do to
   get a dog?
3. How did Ben jump to the top
   of the palace?
4. Why didn't the king let all the
   children jump to the top of the
   palace?

Strange Bumps

New Words

1. <u>Owl</u> wanted to sleep.
2. Rosa has a <u>bump</u> on her head.
3. No, she has two <u>bumps</u> on her head.
4. My head is not at the <u>foot</u> of the bed when I sleep.
5. Touch your nose with your <u>left</u> hand.
6. The <u>blanket</u> is on the bed.
7. The bird made a <u>strange</u> noise.
8. We <u>moved</u> to this city.
9. This is my <u>right</u> hand.

Strange Bumps

Arnold Lobel

Owl was in bed.
"I will go to sleep," he said.
Then Owl saw two bumps under
the blanket at the foot of his bed.
"What can those strange bumps
be?" said Owl.

Owl put up the blanket.
He looked down into the bed.
He could see just black.
Owl wanted to sleep, but he could
not.

"What if those two strange
bumps get big when I sleep?
That would not be nice," said
Owl.

Owl moved his right foot up
and down.
The bump on the right moved up
and down.
"One of those bumps moved!"
said Owl.

Owl moved his left foot up and
down.
The left bump moved up and
down.
"That left bump moved, too!" said
Owl.

Owl let the blanket fall from
his bed.
The bumps were not there.
At the foot of the bed, Owl could
see just his two feet.

"But this is not good," said
Owl.
"I will put the blanket back on."
And he did.

When he did, he saw the two
bumps.
"Those bumps are back!" said
Owl.
"Bumps, bumps, bumps!
I can't sleep!"

Owl hopped up and down on
his bed.
"Where are you?
What are you?" he said.
With a big noise, the bed went
down.

Owl went down.
"I will let those two strange
bumps sit on my bed," said Owl.
"Let them get big if they wish.
I will sleep right here where
there are no bumps."

And that is what he did.

Answer these questions.
1. What did Owl see in his bed?
2. What was under the blanket?
3. How did Owl get to sleep?

Tick
Tock
Clock

Tick tock,
tick tock,
something's hiding
in the clock,
a thing that makes
a ticking sound
and helps the hands
go round and round,
a thing that can't
be very tall
to fit inside
a place that small.
Tick tock,
tick tock,
something's hiding
in the clock.

Jack Prelutsky

When Will the Show Be On?

5:00

2 Animals in the Sea

Travel under the sea and get a good look at some big fish.

4 On Stage

The play today will be *The Clue behind the Old Clock.*

5:30

2 Weather

Will it rain?
This show will let you know.

4 At the Zoo

See a lion and a seal in this show from the city zoo.

Word List

ACKNOWLEDGMENTS

Grateful acknowledgment is given for permission to reprint the following copyrighted material:

"The Big Jump" from *The Big Jump and Other Stories* by Benjamin Elkin. Copyright ©1958 Benjamin Elkin. Adapted by permission of Random House, Inc.

"Chicken Forgets" from *Chicken Forgets* by Miska Miles. Text copyright ©1976 by Miska Miles. By permission of Little, Brown and Company in association with the Atlantic Monthly Press.

"The Furry Ones" from *Feathered Ones and Furry* by Aileen Fisher. Copyright ©1971 by Aileen Fisher. By permission of Harper & Row, Publishers, Inc.

"Go Away, Dog" by Joan L. Nodset. Copyright ©1963 by Joan L. Nodset. Adaptation by permission of Harper & Row, Publishers, Inc.

"Is There a Place?" from *See My Lovely Poison Ivy* by Lillian Moore. Copyright ©1975 by Lillian Moore. Reprinted with the permission of Atheneum Publishers.

"Mr. Pyme" from *The Little Hill* by Harry Behn. Copyright ©1949 by Harry Behn, renewed 1977 by Alice L. Behn. Reprinted by permission of Harcourt Brace Jovanovich, Inc.

"Pete, the Wet Pet" by Catherine Chase. Copyright ©1981 by Daniel Weiner. By permission of Daniel Weiner.

"Sea Frog, City Frog" adapted with permission of Macmillan Publishing Co., Inc., from *Sea Frog, City Frog* by Dorothy O. Van Woerkom. Copyright ©1975 by Dorothy O. Van Woerkom.

"Strange Bumps" (text and art) from *Owl at Home* by Arnold Lobel. Copyright ©1975 by Arnold Lobel. By permission of Harper & Row, Publishers, Inc.

"Tick Tock Clock" from *Rainy Rainy Saturday* by Jack Prelutsky. Copyright ©1980 by Jack Prelutsky. By permission of Greenwillow Books (A Division of William Morrow & Co.).

"You" from *All That Sunlight* by Charlotte Zolotow. Copyright ©1967 by Charlotte Zolotow. By permission of Harper & Row, Publishers, Inc.

Grateful acknowledgment is made to the following for illustrations, photographs, and reproductions on the pages indicated:

Walt Anderson/Tom Stack & Associates 25; Animals Animals/Robert Maier 27; John M. Beals 203; Gwen Connelly 62-71; Dr. E. R. Degginger 10-14, 25, 26; Linda Edwards title page, copyright page, 8, 36, 74, 114, 162; Carolyn Bowser Ewing 82-86, 164, 172; Elizabeth Fong 38-42, 124-130; Gayla Taylor Goodell 73, 113, 161, 204; Pat Hoggan 56-60, 102-111, 140-148, 150-159; Roger F. Huebner 112; Christa Kieffer 116-122; L. Linkhart 25, 28; Arnold Lobel 194-202; Judith McClung/FPG International 24; Elizabeth Miles 50-54; Terra Muzick 132-138; Vera Rosenberry 44-48; Robert Schwartz/FPG International 24, 27; Linda Simmons 30-34; Robert C. Simpson/Tom Stack & Associates 24; Philip Smith 76-80, 182-192; Tom Stack/Tom Stack & Associates 23, 28; Rachel Thompson 24, 27; Ron West 23; Mike Wimmer 22, 174-180; Jane Yamada 72, 96-100, 160; Julie Young 16-20, 35, 88-94.